BECAUSE OF
THE CROSS

by
Beverly Courrege

RIVER
OAK

PUBLISHING

Because of the Cross
ISBN 1-58919-300-8
Copyright © 2001 by Beverly Courrege

Published by RiverOak Publishing
P.O. Box 700143
Tulsa, Oklahoma 74170-0143

INTRODUCTION

What does the Cross of Christ mean to you? Is it a symbol of death? A symbol of life? Does it represent victory and hope? Does it remind you of the price that Jesus Christ paid for each one of us? Does it remind you that He came to earth as a man, to die for the sins of all men, and then rose from the dead three days later? Do you believe that true life begins with the Cross?

It is my prayer that within the pages of this book you will discover the daily work of the Cross. Because Christ died on the Cross there is eternal salvation and abundance of blessings for all those that find Him. Think often of the Cross. Focus on it. Find the encouragement, strength, and promise it gives us. These pages contain just a few of the innumerable blessings and truths that we have *Because of the Cross*. I hope above all that you encounter His great love for you. All thanks and praise to the One who paid the ultimate debt.

In Him,

Beverly Courrege

I HAVE TREASURE IN HEAVEN.

Rejoice in that day and leap for joy,
because great is your reward in heaven.
—LUKE 6:23 NIV

All I have seen teaches me to trust
the Creator for all I have not seen.
—Ralph Waldo Emerson

In a rural community a couple purchased a little home. The previous owner, now deceased, had owned a local movie theatre for decades. While remodeling, the old wallpaper was torn away to reveal treasure hidden within the walls. Vintage movie posters had been used for insulation throughout the entire house. One was worth a small fortune!

Treasure had surrounded the previous owner and sadly he missed it. Sadly, many souls will also miss the treasure of heaven.

BECAUSE OF THE CROSS WE CAN HAVE TRUE RICHES GREATER THAN ANYTHING ON EARTH.

Heaven's treasure is found the moment we make our decision for Christ, our old self is torn away, and the new is revealed! Don't miss it!

I CAN LOVE OTHERS.

Be devoted to one another in brotherly love;
give preference to one another in honor; not lagging
behind in diligence, fervent in spirit, serving the Lord.
—ROMANS 12:10,11 NASB

By this all men will know that you are
my disciples, if you love one another.
—JOHN 13:35 NIV

Love is most divine when it loves according
to needs, and not according to merit.
—George MacDonald

The love we have for our spouses, children, parents, families, and friends is often a love based on who they are, what they mean to us, and how they make us feel. The Cross changes that love. It becomes a deeper, unconditional love that loves even when those we are closest to hurt us or make mistakes. It loves at all times . . . in all things . . . regardless of how we feel.

BECAUSE OF THE CROSS WE CAN HAVE THAT SAME LOVE FOR OTHERS WHO TOUCH OUR LIVES, OFTEN FROM A DISTANCE.

We can love the ungrateful, the unfair, the unjust, the imprisoned, the lonely, the homeless, the liar, the cheater, the thief, the murderer, the abuser, the adulterer, the addict, the disgruntled, the opinionated, the unlovely, the unloved.

Only through the Cross is it possible to love . . . and be loved . . . unconditionally.

EASTER IS EVERY DAY.

Christ also suffered. He died once for
the sins of all us guilty sinners, although he
himself was innocent of any sin at any time,
that he might bring us safely home to God.
But though his body died, his spirit lived on.
—1 PETER 3:18 TLB

The dripping blood our only drink, the bloody
flesh our only food: in spite of which we like to
think that we are sound, substantial flesh and blood.
Again, in spite of that, we call this Friday good.
—T. S. Eliot

The same Christ who walked the earth 2000 years ago.

The same Christ who performed miracles, healed the sick, and cast out demons.

The same Christ who loved the unlovable.

The same Christ who forgave the sinner.

The same Christ who taught His disciples.

The same Christ who was unjustly despised and convicted.

The same Christ who hung dying on a Cross one dark and terrible Friday.

The same Christ who rose from the dead three days later.

This same Christ is in the world today.

BECAUSE OF THE VICTORY OF THE CROSS, THE JOY OF EASTER IS EVERY DAY.

THERE IS HOPE
FOR THE FUTURE.

May the God of hope fill you with all joy and peace
as you trust in him, so that you may overflow
with hope by the power of the Holy Spirit.
—ROMANS 15:13 NIV

"Hope" is the thing with feathers—
That perches in the soul—
And sings the tunes without the words—
And never stops—at all.
—Emily Dickinson

In the game of T-ball little guys and girls stand ready to hit a baseball perched on a T-stand. All they have to do is swing the bat and knock the ball off the stand. Incredibly, many of these little folks swing and miss a perfectly still ball. Yet, they continue to swing with the hope that someday they will hit that ball. Perhaps more incredibly, some of these little guys grow up to be professional baseball players, their greatest hope realized!

Just as these children's hope is steadfast, so is the hope we have as believers. This future hope alights in our souls when we first believe. The full potential of our hope for the future is realized as we stand at the Cross and "connect" with it.

STEP UP TO THE CROSS!
YOU CAN'T MISS!

I HAVE SOMETHING TO SMILE ABOUT.

. . . and so He will make you happy and give you something to smile about.
—JOB 8:21 CEV

The year's at the spring and day's at the morn;
Morning's at seven; the hillside's dew-pearled;
The lark's on the wing; the snail's on the thorn;
God's in his heaven—all's right with the world!
—Robert Browning

Do you have favorite things? Picnics, an ocean view, thunderstorms, snow falling, my husband and children laughing, sunsets, yellow roses, the melancholy tones of a piano, a soprano's song, a note from a friend, a baby's special scent, surprise parties, books on tape, long naps, searching scripture, a snow goose, a good recipe, a beautiful garden, original artwork, soft candlelight . . . these are a few of my favorite things.

BECAUSE OF THE CROSS, GOD IS SMILING DOWN ON ME FROM HEAVEN.

Knowing this gives me a reason to smile too, not just at my favorite things, but in "all things!" Is God smiling down on you?

I CAN HAVE ETERNAL LIFE.

"This is indeed the will of my Father, that all who see
the Son and believe in him may have eternal life;
and I will raise them up on the last day."
—JOHN 6:40 NRSV

For the great hereafter I trust in the infinite love
of God as expressed in the life and death
of our Lord and Savior Jesus Christ.
—Josiah Gilbert Holland

The most significant achievement of the Cross is eternal life. When Adam and Eve sinned we inherited eternal death. Incredibly, God said, "I still love them. Let's give them a second chance." Therefore, in His perfect love God made the ultimate sacrifice by sending His Son to die for every sin—past, present, and future.

ONCE WE KNOW IN OUR HEARTS AND BELIEVE, IF THE NEXT BREATH WE TAKE IS OUR LAST, EVERYTHING WE RECEIVE BECAUSE OF THE CROSS CULMINATES IN ETERNITY.

Our defining moment is to believe that Jesus Christ, Son of God and Son of Man, died on the Cross for each one of us so we can have eternal life with Him.

I CAN BE STILL.

You who still the noise of the seas, the noise
of their waves, and the tumult of the peoples.
—PSALM 65:7 NKJV

Certainly work is not always required of a man.
There is such a thing as a sacred idleness—the
cultivation of which is now fearfully neglected.
—George MacDonald

Being still is not surfing TV channels with a remote.
Being still is not mindless reading.
Being still is not sitting at a red light.
Being still is not turning off the ringer of the phone.
Being still is not watching a sunset.
Being still is not lingering over lunch.
Being still is not sipping coffee.
Being still is not taking a nap.
Being still is not holding your beloved's hand.
Being still is not keeping your eye on the ball.
Being still is not sitting quietly in a church pew.

BEING STILL IS SITTING AT THE FOOT OF THE CROSS.

ALL MY NEEDS ARE MET.

And it is he who will supply all your needs
from his riches in glory, because of
what Christ Jesus has done for us.
—PHILIPPIANS 4:19 TLB

Be anxious for nothing, prayerful
for everything, thankful for anything.
—D. L. Moody

The Lord that watches over the sparrow is committed to watch over us as well. We all have basic physical, emotional, and spiritual needs. Our world is filled with endless opportunities and material blessings that past generations could not have imagined. Yet even today our faith can still be challenged to trust God for the most basic physical needs of shelter, food, and clothing.

BECAUSE OF THE CROSS GOD HAS PROMISED TO SUPPLY EVERYTHING THAT I NEED.

Not only does He meet our physical needs, but He meets our spiritual and emotional needs as well. Christ died so we can have the riches of God's gifts of grace, joy, emotional well-being, and life. Christ paid the ultimate price on the Cross so that I would not have to . . . in Him all my needs are met.

THERE IS A LIGHT
IN THE DARKNESS.

But you are a chosen generation, a royal priesthood,
a holy nation, His own special people, that you
may proclaim the praises of Him who called you
out of darkness into His marvelous light.
—1 PETER 2:9 NKJV

If we do not radiate the light of Christ
around us, the sense of the darkness
that prevails in the world will increase.
—Mother Teresa

Have you ever seen a night so dark you thought you could sleep with your eyes open? While on a weekend retreat, a friend and I experienced such a night as we walked through the woods on our way to a bonfire.

I was holding a feeble excuse for a flashlight. With almost every step along our path we were tripping over limbs and rocks and potholes! As a result, the limited light we had was bouncing uselessly off our path, into the trees and the total blackness surrounding us.

Finally, at a turn in the path we stopped to try and compose ourselves. Suddenly, a great light illuminated the area around us. Other friends had caught up to us and their light source was like a truck's high beam!

THERE IS A LIGHT GREATER THAN I CAN DESCRIBE. THE LIGHT OF THE CROSS.

There, continually shining, Christ illuminates the limbs, rocks, and potholes as we walk with Him in a dark world.

I HAVE REASON
TO REJOICE.

*"Rejoice in the Lord always—delight, gladden
yourselves in Him; again I say, Rejoice!"*
—PHILIPPIANS 4:4 AMP

A child of God should be a visible
beatitude for joy and happiness, and
a living doxology for gratitude and adoration.
—Charles Haddon Spurgeon

Rejoice, dear one, rejoice! Rejoice when the plumbing breaks because you are blessed with a home! "Rejoice!" again He says, "Rejoice!" when all your children have piano, soccer, and cheerleading practice on the same night! Rejoice in the special gift that your children are and the many opportunities they have to grow and learn.

Rejoice! Rejoice! Not only for those things we can see but for the things we cannot.

Rejoice, because sorrow can change to joy. Rejoice, because guilt can be eliminated by forgiveness. Rejoice, because worry can change to peace. Rejoice, because anger can change to love.

REJOICE IN THE KNOWLEDGE THAT BECAUSE OF THE CROSS, DEATH IN THIS LIFE BRINGS LIFE EVERLASTING.

I CAN BE A PERSON OF INTEGRITY.

But as for me, I will walk in mine integrity:
redeem me, and be merciful unto me.
—PSALM 26:11 KJV

In everything set them an example by doing what is
good. In your teaching show integrity, seriousness
and soundness of speech that cannot be condemned.
—TITUS 2:7,8 NIV

Give us the man of integrity, on whom we know
we can thoroughly depend; who will stand firm when
others fail; the friend, faithful and true; the adviser,
honest and fearless; the adversary, just and chivalrous;
such an one is a fragment of the Rock of Ages.

—Arthur P. Stanley

Is there a person in your life who will keep a commitment no matter what happens? Someone who always seems to listen attentively and gives judicious advice? Do you have a friend who can help you discern right from wrong? Someone who not only would never lie to you, but would not even consider "stretching the truth" just a tiny little bit? Is there someone you would depend on in a crisis? Would you trust them with your life?

WOULD SOMEONE DESCRIBE
YOU AS THIS KIND OF FRIEND?
WALK IN THE INTEGRITY
OF THE CROSS.

I CAN WALK AND TALK WITH GOD.

*Because the Lord is my Shepherd, I have
everything I need! He lets me rest in the meadow
grass and leads me beside the quiet streams.
Even when walking through the dark valley
of death I will not be afraid, for you are close
beside me, guarding, guiding all the way.*
—PSALM 23: 1–2, 4 TLB

When we walk in the Lord's presence, everything
we see, hear, touch, or taste reminds us of him.
—Henri J. Nouwen

I spent the day with God today. His breeze blew across my face and kissed my brow, and His sun warmed me. I knelt in His garden to pick His fragrant rose. The dog He gave me ran up to lick my cheek and then darted off to chase His butterfly. The moisture of His rain from the night before still lingered on His blades of grass beneath my feet. Hearing laughter, I turned to see the family He gave me . . . and I am reminded once more that my life is His.

DID YOU SPEND YOUR DAY WITH GOD TODAY?

THERE IS NO NEED TO WORRY.

Humble yourselves, therefore, under God's mighty hand, that he may lift you up in due time. Cast all your anxiety on him because he cares for you.
—1 PETER 5:6,7 NIV

O God give me the serenity to accept the things
I cannot change, courage to change the things
I can, and wisdom to know the difference.
—St. Francis of Assisi

Stop pacing! Are you wringing your hands? Shaking your head? Clenching your fists? Is your brow furrowed? Are you grinding your teeth? Why bite your nails?

Are you having a bad day? There is nothing you will face that God can't handle. We have a loving, caring Father who wants to carry our burdens for us. Let go of the need to be in control and fall to your knees. Humble yourself and let God have complete control of your life.

Remember Christ's worst day. He suffered unbearable pain and endured all of our worst days for us on the Cross! Why worry when you already have what you need?

PLACE ALL OF YOUR TROUBLES AT THE FOOT OF THE CROSS.

I HAVE REFUGE.

He who dwells in the shelter of the Most
High will rest in the shadow of the Almighty.
I will say of the Lord, "He is my refuge and
my fortress, my God, in whom I trust."
—PSALM 91:1,2 NIV

How often we look upon God as our last and
feeblest resource! We go to him because we
have no where else to go. And then we learn
that the storms of life have driven us, not
upon the rocks, but into the desired haven.
—George MacDonald

I put a gecko (also known as a live caricature of a pre-historic lizard!) out of my house and a little while later, I opened the door and it came scurrying right back into the "refuge" inside. I wondered if this tiny creature reasoned that "in" was safer than "out."

How important it is to know where our safe place is. Whenever I find myself thrust "outside" into the world—either by my own actions or the circumstances I face—I am thankful that the door to my safe haven is always held open by Christ. Are you frightened and tired? Do you need a safe place to rest your soul?

THERE IS NO PLACE SAFER THAN THE REFUGE OF THE CROSS.

I WILL BE A SURVIVOR.

*Because everyone who is a child of God
conquers the world. And this is the victory
that conquers the world—our faith.*
—1 JOHN 5:4 NCV

The strength of man sinks in the hour of trial:
but there doth live a power that
to the battle girdeth the weak.
—Joanna Baille

Are you a victim? There are all kinds of terrible situations and circumstances that can leave a person feeling helpless and victimized . . . physical or emotional abuse, poverty, dysfunctional families, absent or unloving parents, lack of opportunity, severe illness or great physical challenges.

While there may be a legitimate reason to see yourself as a victim, there is an even greater reason to believe you can overcome.

BECAUSE OF THE CROSS, WE DO NOT HAVE TO BE VICTIMS.

Christ overcame at the Cross so you and I, in spite of our weaknesses and circumstances, can be survivors!

I AM SPIRITUALLY ALIVE.

Create in me a clean heart, O God,
and put a new and right spirit within me.
—PSALM 51:10 NRSV

Grant us thy truth to make us free,
And kindling hearts that burn for thee,
Till all thy living altars claim,
One holy light, one heavenly flame.
—Oliver Wendell Holmes

Have you ever considered the amount of effort we spend each day living our lives? We must decide what to eat. What to wear. Which car to drive. Where to work. What house to buy. What school to attend. What gym to work out in. Where to travel. What sport to play. What to watch on TV. What goal to achieve. These decisions often determine the quality of our daily lives.

BECAUSE OF THE CROSS, OUR SPIRITS ARE ALIVE.

Yet do we spend the same amount of effort in making decisions that improve the quality of our spiritual lives? What nourishment has your spirit received today? What encouragement? What growth? What direction? All of this and more are found at the Cross.

I HAVE A CHOICE.

. . .I have set before you life and death,
blessing and cursing: therefore choose life,
that both thou and thy seed may live.
—DEUTERONOMY 30:19 KJV

Between two evils, choose neither;
between two goods, choose both.
—Tryon Edwards

I have a choice to make a difference
   or miss an opportunity.
I have a choice to speak a loving word
   or a word that hurts.
I have a choice to build a relationship or to destroy it.
I have a choice to be content or to complain.
I have a choice to show compassion or to judge.
I have a choice to love or to hate.
I have a choice to bless or to curse.
I have a choice to avoid temptation or to yield to it.
I have a choice to understand or to condemn.
I have a choice of life in the Cross or death.

YOU ALSO HAVE A CHOICE.
CHOOSE THE CROSS.
CHOOSE LIFE!

IT IS WELL WITH MY SOUL.

Thou wilt keep him in perfect peace, whose mind is stayed on thee: because he trusteth in thee.
—ISAIAH 26:3 KJV

When peace like a river attendeth my way,
When sorrows like sea-billows roll;
Whatever my lot, Thou hast taught me to say,
"It is well, it is well with my soul."
—Horatio G. Spafford / Philip P. Bliss

Soul peace—the constant and unfailing peace that lies deep within the soul, no matter what comes. God tells us the kind of peace He gives to us is beyond our ability to understand. We cannot comprehend how this soul peace guards our hearts and minds against hurt, anger, depression, envy, temptation, guilt, fear, doubt, rebellion, frustration, and worry . . . it just does.

Are you fearfully facing a storm?

FIND THE ASSURANCE AND PEACE
THAT ONLY GOD CAN GIVE . . .
AT THE CROSS OF CHRIST.

I HAVE JOY FOR THE JOURNEY.

Though you have not seen him, you love him;
and even though you do not see him now, you
believe in him and are filled with an inexpressible
and glorious joy, for you are receiving the goal
of your faith, the salvation of your souls.
—1 PETER 1:8,9 NIV

Grief can take care of itself, but to get the full value
of joy you must have someone to share it with.
—Mark Twain

People who were at the Seattle Special Olympics a few years ago are still telling the story of nine very special contestants who finished the 100-yard dash.

The gun sounded and they began their 100-yard journey . . . all except one little boy who tripped, tumbling head-over-heels a couple of times, bringing the inevitable tears.

The other eight, off to a successful start, heard the boy crying, slowed, and looked back. Every one of them turned and went back to the boy. A little girl with Down's Syndrome bent down, kissed him and said, "This will make it better." Then all nine contestants linked arms and finished their journey to the finish line together.

Do you have joy for the journey?

TURN AROUND AND BRING OTHERS ALONG WITH YOU.

THERE IS ONE
WHO LISTENS.

I cried unto the LORD with my voice,
and he heard me out of his holy hill.
—PSALM 3:4 KJV

We cannot too often think there is
a never-sleeping eye, which reads
the heart, and registers our thoughts.
—Francis Bacon

A few years ago I ran into a "celebrity" acquaintance of mine and friends that were with me thought it would make a fun photo-op. As we stood smiling at the camera the acquaintance turned to me and asked, "Am I supposed to know you?" Prompting her with a few particulars to jar her memory of our previous acquaintance, she might have had a vague recollection . . . if she had been listening.

The Lord needs no such prompting to recognize my voice, spoken or unspoken. The voice of my supplications is always heard.

BECAUSE OF THE CROSS HE
KNOWS MY NAME, MY VOICE,
AND LISTENS TO MY EVERY WORD.

HEAVEN IS MY HOME.

Now we know that if the earthly tent we live in is
destroyed, we have a building from God, an eternal
house in heaven, not built by human hands.
—2 CORINTHIANS 5:1 NIV

God's thoughts, his will, his love, his judgments are
all man's home. To think his thoughts, to choose
his will, to love his loves, to judge his judgments,
and thus to know that he is in us, is to be at home.
—George MacDonald

Think for a minute about your "earthly tent." We probably think about our homes more than once or twice a day. Is it too small? Too big? Is it updated or does it need some remodeling? Is it clean, or in need of some elbow grease? It seems that something always needs to be fixed, doesn't it?

How often do we think of our home in heaven? I, for one, am excited that God is preparing a special place for me so magnificent that it is beyond anything I can imagine here on earth. If I look around my "earthly tent" and find it lacking, I only have to think of the Cross and look at my surroundings through His eyes. It's temporary!

BECAUSE OF THE CROSS, I HAVE A HOME IN HEAVEN RIGHT NOW AND FOREVER.

What a wonderful dwelling place we have with Him. Home is truly where the heart is!

FRIENDS CAN BE FOREVER.

But it is you, a man like myself, my companion,
my close friend, with whom I once enjoyed
sweet fellowship as we walked with
the throng at the house of God.
—PSALM 55:13,14 NIV

A true friend . . . advises justly, assists readily,
adventures boldly, takes all patiently, defends
courageously, and continues a friend unchangeably.
—William Penn

Recently a tragic death brought together many friends from all over the country who had attended church together twenty-five years ago. Time and distance vanished instantly as faithful friends came together to share the pain of loss and the fulfilled promise of never-ending life with God.

Whether separated by death, distance, time, or change, friendship need not be limited to our earthly lives. What a celebration, when one day we will enter the house of God to enjoy joyous reunions and sweet fellowship.

THE BOND OF FRIENDSHIP
THAT IS UNITED IN THE
CROSS LASTS FOREVER.

CHRIST CAN LIVE THROUGH ME.

*I have been crucified with Christ and I no longer
live, but Christ lives in me. The life I live in
the body, I live by faith in the Son of God,
who loved me and gave himself for me.*
—GALATIANS 2:20 NIV

Every occupation, plan, and work of man, to be
truly successful, must be done under the direction
of Christ, in union with his will, from love
to him, and, in dependence on his power.
—Friedrich Max Muller

One of my friends says my home has "drive-up" appeal. We have lived in our home for more than twenty years and every blade of grass, garden flower, and tree has been planted by my husband and me. I think what makes driving up to our home so appealing is that everything we have planted is maturing.

As believers mature, they too have "drive-up" appeal. Christ's presence in a life becomes even more evident with time. Life in Christ becomes appealing to others when they can see Christ living through someone completely dependent upon Him.

A LIFE THAT BECOMES ONE WITH "DRIVE-UP" APPEAL CAN ONLY BEGIN AT THE CROSS. START TODAY!

PRAYER IS POWERFUL.

Jesus answered them, "Truly I tell you, if you have faith and do not doubt, not only will you do what has been done to the fig tree, but even if you say to this mountain, 'Be lifted up and thrown into the sea,' it will be done. Whatever you ask for in prayer with faith, you will receive."
—MATTHEW 21:21,22 NRSV

This is the assurance we have in approaching God: that if we ask anything according to his will, he hears us.
—1 JOHN 5:14 NIV

I know no blessing so small as to be reasonably expected without prayer, nor any so great but may be attained by it.

—Robert South

Prayer is powerful when we pray for the unexpected or the impossible and believe that it will happen. Prayer is powerful when it is selfless. Prayer is powerful when we let God say "no." Prayer is powerful when we pray for those that God leads us to pray for. Prayer is powerful when we respond to what God shows us to do.

Life-changing prayer is only possible because of the Cross. Because Christ died for our sins, we can communicate openly with the Father. He always hears and His heart is moved when His children pray.

BECAUSE OF THE CROSS, OUR PRAYERS CAN MOVE MOUNTAINS.

I HAVE TRUE WEALTH.

Oh, what a wonderful God we have!
How great are his wisdom and knowledge and riches!
For everything comes from God alone.
Everything lives by his power, and everything
is for his glory. To him be glory evermore.
—ROMANS 11:33,36 TLB

Shall wealth be all of worldly things, and richness
gained through gathered wares? Or rather found
in silent dawns, the reverence of evening prayers?
—A. S. Leigh

It has been documented that in Dallas, Texas, every day during the month of June, 2000, at least one million-dollar-plus home was sold—many of which were paid for in cash. Wow! In a society where affluence seems to be the rule rather than the exception, it can be a challenge to keep our eyes focused on God.

Material wealth can become hazardous if it becomes more desirable than the true wealth of the Cross. Peace, joy, faith, acceptance, grace, mercy, wisdom, and life everlasting—these are just a few of the countless blessings God gives his children.

HOLD FAST TO WHAT WE CANNOT ATTAIN ON OUR OWN, THE TRUE RICHES OF THE CROSS!

I KNOW THE SECRET OF A HAPPY LIFE.

But life is worth nothing unless I use it for doing the work assigned me by the Lord Jesus— the work of telling others the Good News about God's mighty kindness and love.

—ACTS 20:24 TLB

To find joy in another's joy is the secret of happiness.
—George Bernanos

A local radio station awarded a recent contest winner tickets for a special concert. The winner's excitement was multiplied when she learned she was receiving ten extra tickets to share with friends and family.

We experience great joy when we find faith in Christ and receive His salvation, but our happiness is multiplied only when we share our discovery with others. The secret to a happy life is finding every opportunity to tell others about the love that God has for them . . . there is no limit to the number of people that you can include.

SHARE THE GOOD NEWS OF THE CROSS!

I HAVE CONFIDENCE.

But Christ as a Son over His own house,
whose house we are if we hold fast the confidence
and the rejoicing of the hope firm to the end.
—HEBREWS 3:6 NKJV

Do not, therefore, abandon that confidence
of yours; it brings a great reward.
—HEBREWS 10:35 NRSV

The Christian has greatly the advantage
of the unbeliever, having everything
to gain and nothing to lose.
—George Gordon Noel Byron

True confidence is a knowing expectation that something is going to happen. We have confidence that if we flip a switch the light will come on. We have confidence that spring will come after a long winter. We have confidence that there will be a new day tomorrow.

Because of the Cross, we have an even greater confidence that God's promises are true. We have confidence that He loves us. We have confidence that He is working on our behalf. We have confidence that we can successfully accomplish what He calls us to do. We have confidence that we are members of His "house." We have confidence that we will spend eternity with Him.

Do you struggle with uncertainty?

FIND YOUR CONFIDENCE AT THE CROSS . . . AND DON'T LET GO!

I AM NEVER ALONE.

And be sure of this—that I am with you
always, even to the end of the world.
—MATTHEW 28:20 TLB

God is great, and therefore he will be sought:
he is good, and therefore he will be found.
—John Jay

There are two kinds of alone—solitude and loneliness. Solitude is withdrawing, passing time in isolation. There are some that choose to spend their entire lives in solitude . . . while others never seem to have a minute to themselves. Loneliness is an overwhelming feeling of emptiness and abandonment that can be experienced even while surrounded by those we love.

BECAUSE OF THE CROSS, WE ARE NEVER ALONE.

Even in solitude, Christ is with us. Time spent "alone" with Him can energize, uplift, enrich, and strengthen our lives. Because of the Cross, we never need to feel lonely or abandoned. Even in the darkest moments He is with us, ready to give love and encouragement, to talk and listen. Christ has promised, and it is true . . . He is with us always.

I AM FORGIVEN.

*If we confess our sins, he is faithful and just
and will forgive us our sins and purify us
from all unrighteousness.*
—1 JOHN 1:9 NIV

*He does not treat us as our sins deserve or
repay us according to our iniquities. As far
as the east is from the west, so far has
he removed our transgressions from us.*
—PSALM 103:10,12 NIV

When God forgives He forgets. He buries
our sins in the sea and puts a sign on the
bank saying, "No Fishing Allowed."
—Corrie ten Boom

Because of the Cross, God not only puts our past sins far from us . . . He forgets them! Does sin haunt your life? Do you struggle to forget past wrongs? Be encouraged!

BECAUSE OF THE CROSS
WE CAN CONFESS OUR SINS
AND ASK FOR FORGIVENESS,
AND HE ALWAYS FORGIVES.

God will not remind you of your old self . . . in Him you are a new creation.

Christ paid the ultimate price for our sins once and for all on the Cross. Don't let the mistakes of the past hinder your walk with Him today. Don't let the work of the Cross be in vain . . . experience His cleansing forgiveness and let go of the past.

MY LIFE IS FULL
OF PURPOSE.

For we are God's workmanship, created in
Christ Jesus to do good works, which God
prepared in advance for us to do.
—EPHESIANS 2:10 NIV

The man without a purpose is like a ship without a
rudder—a waif, a nothing, a no man. Have a purpose
in life, and, having it, throw such strength of mind
and muscle into your work as God has given you.
—Thomas Carlyle

"I don't really know who I am." "He's trying to find himself." "She's reinventing herself." Do these phrases sound familiar? Tragically, many people struggle with frustration, misdirection, emptiness, and confusion as they search for their true reason for being.

Do you feel lost in life? God knows just where you are . . . and where you are supposed to be. He has created you for a specific and unique purpose.

THERE IS A WONDERFUL PLAN FOR YOUR LIFE THAT CAN ONLY BE FOUND IN THE CROSS OF CHRIST.

We can know who we are, we are no longer lost, and we are reinvented in the Cross!

JOY IS MY STRENGTH.

The LORD is my strength and my song; he has become my salvation. Shouts of joy and victory resound in the tents of the righteous.
—PSALM 118:14,15 NIV

Joy is the characteristic by which God uses us to remake the distressing into the desired, the discarded into the creative. Joy is prayer—Joy is strength—Joy is love—Joy is a net of love by which you can catch souls.
—Mother Teresa

The joy of my salvation is my strength.

It is a joy that makes my heart glad.

It is a joy that sets me apart from others.

It is a joy that witnesses to the world.

It is a joy that makes me want to sing and shout!

It is a joy that delights in spiritual things.

It is a joy that causes me to smile at the future.

It is a joy that directs my gratitude,
   praise, and adoration toward heaven.

It is a joy that strengthens my spirit.

IT IS THE JOY OF THE CROSS.

ALL THINGS ARE POSSIBLE.

Jesus looked at them and said, "With man this is impossible, but with God all things are possible."
—MATTHEW 19:26 NIV

(Alice to the White Queen)
"One can't believe impossible things."

"I daresay you haven't had much practice," said the Queen. "When I was your age, I always did it half-an-hour a day. Why sometimes I've believed as many as six impossible things before breakfast."
—Lewis Carroll

Countless stories are told of men and women who defied their human limitations and achieved the "impossible." Joni Eareckson Tada, completely paralyzed in a diving accident, uses her mouth to draw and paint with great skill. Helen Keller, deaf and blind from childhood, achieved high levels of education and influence. Beethoven composed some of his most well known works *after* becoming completely deaf. Mere men believed they could walk on the moon . . . and did it.

How much more can we accomplish with God?

BECAUSE OF THE CROSS
THERE ARE NO LIMITATIONS.

What impossible thing do you need today? With God, all things are possible.

I CAN MAKE
A DIFFERENCE.

*We always thank God for all of you, mentioning you
in our prayers. We continually remember before our
God and Father your work produced by faith, your
labor prompted by love, and your endurance
inspired by hope in our Lord Jesus Christ.*
—1 THESSALONIANS 1:2,3 NIV

No act falls fruitless; none can tell how
vast its powers may be; nor what results,
enfolded dwell within it silently.
—Edward George Bulwer-Lytton

For fifteen years I served in the women's ministry at my church. During that time, there were two women who were committed to pray for me on a regular basis. What a blessing it was when these women would ask me every week what they could pray about for me. What a difference it made in my life to see those prayers answered, and to have the comfort of knowing that someone was always remembering me and lifting me up before God.

BECAUSE OF THE CROSS, WHAT MAY SEEM INSIGNIFICANT OR GO UNNOTICED CAN CHANGE LIVES.

In both the big ways and small, we can make a difference in the lives of others.

SIN HAS NO POWER OVER ME.

For sin shall not any longer exert dominion over you,
since now you are not under Law as slaves, but under
Grace—as subjects to God's favor and mercy.
—ROMANS 6:14 AMP

All the sin that has darkened human life and
saddened human history began in believing
a falsehood; all the power of Christianity to
make men holy is associated with believing truth.
—John Albert Broadus

In a new and perfect world the deception of a serpent would forever change the course of history. Because of Adam's sin, every man and woman would be born with a sinful nature that would separate them from a holy and righteous God. After all this time, Adam and Eve's adversary, Satan, is still around! He continues to do everything he can to deceive people and keep them separated from God's love and grace.

BECAUSE OF THE CROSS WE HAVE POWER OVER SIN AND SATAN'S DECEPTIONS.

Jesus came into our sinful world to die, not just to give us eternal life, but also to free us from the control of our old sinful natures. The good news is sin does not have to rule your life. Believe the truth and receive the victory of the Cross!

I AM HEALED.

He himself bore our sins in his body on the
cross, so that, free from sins, we might live for
righteousness; by his wounds you have been healed.
—1 PETER 2:24 NRSV

Thou, O Christ, art all I want,
More than all in Thee I find;
Raise the fallen, cheer the faint,
Heal the sick and lead the blind.
—Charles Wesley / Simeon B. Marsh

Are you in pain? Does your heart hurt inside?
Are you trapped by addiction? Are you asking,
"Why me?" Are you just hoping to make it through
this day and yet dreading tomorrow? Do you long to
be free from your suffering?

If you need healing, there is One who was born to
die for all of your pain . . . yesterday, today, and
tomorrow. He died for the distress of illness. He died
for the tears of heartache. He died for the anguish of
depression, grief, and sorrow. He died for the
bondage of sin. He died so you can face tomorrow
with joy. Trust Him for victory over your affliction,
whether here or in eternity.

BY HIS STRIPES WE ARE HEALED.

I CAN WALK IN FREEDOM.

If the Son therefore shall make
you free, ye shall be free indeed.
—JOHN 8:36 KJV

Now we are free, there's no condemnation!
Jesus provides a perfect salvation.
—Phillip F. Bliss

At last! Thank God, Almighty, I am free at last! I am free from the bondage of sin. My spirit is free to soar to His upward call. I am free to be His disciple. I am free to know Him. I am free to love Him. I am free to live my life for Him. I am free from my past. I can be free of temporal tyrannies. I am free to walk in purity. I am free to dwell on spiritual matters. I am free to lead others to Christ. I am free to be all God intends me to be!

BECAUSE OF THE CROSS,
I AM FREE INDEED!

I CAN GIVE MY PROBLEMS TO GOD.

A righteous man may have many troubles,
but the LORD delivers him from them all.
—PSALM 34:19 NIV

"These are the times that try men's souls."
—Thomas Paine

We all have problems. I like to look at them as challenges. While we may feel we have more than our fair share of challenges . . . the truth is all of us have them, no matter how influential, wealthy, beautiful, or intelligent we may be. God never promised us that life would be simple . . . in fact He promised we would have many challenges! The good news is that God is more than able to help us handle them all.

BECAUSE OF THE CROSS, WE NEVER NEED TO FACE A CHALLENGE ALONE.

We can give all of our problems to God, and He will be faithful to deliver us.

I CAN LIVE AN ABUNDANT LIFE.

. . . I am come that they might have life, and that they might have it more abundantly.
—JOHN 10:10 KJV

Give, and it shall be given unto you; good measure, pressed down, and shaken together, and running over, shall men give into your bosom.
—LUKE 6:38 KJV

To value riches is not to be covetous. They are the gift of God, and, like every gift of his, good in themselves, and capable of a good use. But to overvalue riches, to give them a place in the heart which God did not design them to fill, this is covetousness.

—Herman Lincoln Wayland

One evening you visit a five-star restaurant. After quickly reading the menu, you select a favorite dish. You finish the meal . . . eating every bite . . . when suddenly the head chef appears at your table to offer the very best meal in the house. Unfortunately, you are so full that you cannot possibly eat another bite.

In a similar way, we often miss out on the very best that God has for us. It is easy to become "full" of material possessions, status, activities . . . things we think are good. But God has abundant blessings for our lives that He has prepared just for us . . . both material and spiritual.

ABUNDANT LIFE IS ONLY FOUND AT THE CROSS.

I HAVE PEACE IN THE MIDST OF THE STORM.

He got up, rebuked the wind and said to the waves,
"Quiet! Be still!" Then the wind calmed down and
it was completely calm. He said to His disciples,
"Why are you so afraid? Do you still have no faith?"
—MARK 4:39,40 NIV

Character like photography develops in darkness.
—Yousut Charsh

My husband, his friend, and their sons were fishing off the coast of California when a sudden storm engulfed their small vessel. The shore was only twenty miles ahead but even at full throttle the darkness and pouring rain made the distance seem greater. Fortunately, the little boat had a newly installed global positioning system (GPS). Frightened and alarmed, the men nonetheless had faith that the GPS could guide them safely toward shore and shelter. Hope and peace prevailed as the steady beep, beep, beep of the lighted buoy led them safely home.

We can have that same hope and peace in the storms of life.

THE BEACON OF THE CROSS CALMS THE WIND AND WAVES, AND BRINGS US SAFELY TO SHORE EVERY TIME.

I AM GOD'S CHILD.

*Behold, what manner of love the Father
hath bestowed upon us, that we
should be called the sons of God.*
—1 JOHN 3:1 KJV

The only way to realize we are God's children
is to let Christ lead us to our Father.
—Phillips Brooks

Can other people look at you and see that you are a child of God? Does your life reveal Christ to others? I often wonder if people can look at me and see the evidence of my Father. As often as I ask myself this question, I am amazed and encouraged if the answer is yes!

One Saturday at a neighborhood block party, a neighbor I knew of but hadn't met before came up to me and began describing the woes of real estate in our area. When she asked if I had sold the house on the next street I looked at her in confusion. I explained to her that I didn't work in real estate, and then she looked confused. "When I read the listing agent's name on the sign I assumed that was you. You are 'Beverly Christian,' aren't you?" she asked. I guess she knew more about me than I realized!

Do you know your heavenly Father?

HE IS WAITING FOR YOU
AT THE CROSS.

I CAN BE A PERSON OF INFLUENCE.

And she will always be remembered for this deed. The story of what she has done will be told throughout the whole world, wherever the Good News is preached.
—MATTHEW 26:13 TLB

Influence never dies; every act, emotion, look,
and word makes influence tell for good or evil,
happiness or woe, through the long future of eternity.
—Thomas a' Kempis

She said, "Yes!" Cassie Bernall, Columbine High School student, faced a critical decision when a fellow student held a gun in her face that terrible day in April 1999. When the gunman asked "Do you believe in God?" she must have known in an instant that to proclaim her faith in Christ would surely cost her life. In the face of certain death, Cassie said "Yes!" and was killed.

Cassie and others like her are not soon forgotten, and the influence their faith has on the world is not easily measured. Do you wonder what you would do if faced with the same situation? Is the love you have for Christ so strong that not even the threat of death would silence your testimony for Him? When the Cross is visible in our lives we have immeasurable influence on those around us.

CAN OTHERS SEE THE CROSS IN YOU?

I AM BLESSED.

Blessed are those who dwell in your house; they are ever praising you. Blessed are those whose strength is in you, who have set their hearts on pilgrimage.

—PSALM 84:4,5 NIV

The beloved of the Almighty are the rich who
have the humility of the poor, and the poor
who have the magnanimity of the rich.

—Saadi

Blessed is the man who is humble.
Blessed is the man who mourns.
Blessed is the man who hungers
   and thirsts for righteousness.
Blessed is the man who loves others.
Blessed is the man who is merciful.
Blessed is the man who is pure in heart.
Blessed is the man who makes peace.
Blessed is the man who is persecuted
   because of righteousness.
Blessed is the man who builds treasure in heaven.

BLESSED IS THE MAN
WHO FINDS THE CROSS.

I CAN SHARE THE LOVE OF CHRIST.

"As the Father has loved me, so have I loved you.
Now remain in my love. My command is this:
Love each other as I have loved you."
—JOHN 15:9,12 NIV

Therefore be imitators of God, as beloved children,
and live in love, as Christ loved us and gave himself
up for us, a fragrant offering and sacrifice to God.
—EPHESIANS 5:1,2 NRSV

Brotherly love is still the distinguishing
badge of every true Christian.
—Matthew Henry

The love of Christ in us is the world's glimpse of God. How important is it then to fulfill the greatest responsibility that God gives to us . . . to share His love with others? His love can be seen in an old man's shining, joyful face, or in a woman's loving smile. His love can be received through a warm meal or a thoughtful gift. His love can be given by a listening ear, or a compassionate embrace.

CHRIST LOVED US SO MUCH HE PAID THE ULTIMATE PRICE ON THE CROSS.

Having received His love, how can we not give it away?

I AM COMPLETE.

*For in Him dwells all the fullness of the
Godhead bodily; and you are complete in Him,
who is the head of all principality and power.*
—COLOSSIANS 2:9,10 NKJV

To be what we are, and to become what we
are capable of becoming, is the only end of life.
—Robert Louis Stevenson

I am complete because Christ is alive in my heart.
I am complete because God is at work in my life.
I am complete because I am becoming
   what He created me to be.
I am complete because He is growing love, joy,
   peace, patience, kindness, goodness, faith,
   gentleness, and self-control in me.
I am complete because He fills all
   the empty places in my heart.
I am complete because I know Him.

IS YOUR LIFE COMPLETE?

I WON'T BE LEFT BEHIND.

Fight the good fight of the faith. Take hold
of the eternal life to which you were called
when you made your good confession in the
presence of many witnesses . . . I charge you to
keep this command without spot or blame until
the appearing of our Lord Jesus Christ, which
God will bring about in his own time. . . .
—1 TIMOTHY 6:12–14 NIV

The strength and happiness of a man consists in finding
out the way God is going, and going in that way, too.
—Henry Ward Beecher

A recent television commercial shows a group of ballplayers choosing sides. When the teams are complete, and both sides have chosen equally, the inevitable has happened. There is one player too many. One who will not get to play at all. He has been left behind.

When Christ returns for His church, there will be many who are left behind. Unlike the ballplayers, we make the choice to be included.

ALL WE NEED TO DO IS CHOOSE THE CROSS.

Don't be left behind, join His team today!

EVERYTHING I DO IS SIGNIFICANT.

*The sins of some men are obvious, reaching the
place of judgment ahead of them; the sins of others
trail behind them. In the same way, good deeds are
obvious, and even those that are not cannot be hidden.*
—1 TIMOTHY 5:24,25 NIV

The things that Jesus did were of the most menial
and commonplace order, and this is an indication
that it takes all God's power in me to do the most
commonplace things in His way . . . All the ordinary
sordid things of our lives reveal more quickly
than anything what we are made of.
—Oswald Chambers

There is significance in everything we do in life . . . both the extraordinary things and the routine responsibilities. Doing the dishes, preparing meals, folding the laundry, driving car pool, providing for our family, and going to school might seem insignificant, but what would our lives be like if we didn't do these things? Getting married, having children, attending church, the words we speak, the habits we have, the friends we choose, how we spend our money . . . do these things not determine the quality of our lives and those we love?

In the same way, what we *don't* do can be equally significant. What happens to the world around you should you decide not to vote, not to visit an aging loved one, not to listen to your child, not to voice an encouraging word, not to obey the speed limit, not to love your neighbor, not to fulfill God's plan for your life?

BECAUSE OF THE CROSS OUR LIVES
HAVE PURPOSE . . . EVERYTHING
WE DO IS A SIGNIFICANT EXAMPLE
FOR OTHERS TO FOLLOW.

I HAVE NOTHING TO FEAR.

So say with confidence, "The Lord is my helper;
I will not be afraid. What can man do to me?"
—HEBREWS 13:6 NIV

There is a virtuous fear which is the effect
of faith, and a vicious fear which is the product
of doubt and distrust. The former leads to hope
relying on God, in whom we believe; the latter
inclines to despair, as not relying upon God.
—Blaise Pascal

Do you remember those things that used to frighten or intimidate us as children? That bump in the night or the scary "monster" under the bed? The first attempt to ride a bike? The first day at school? Being alone in a dark room at night? A loud thunderstorm? For many of us, daddy was there to calm our fears and help us face the unknown.

How much more do we have a loving heavenly Father who quiets our fears? Whether we face a physical threat, or fear the unknown ahead, He is always there.

BECAUSE OF THE CROSS WE HAVE AN AWESOME AND POWERFUL "DADDY!"

What is there to fear?

I CAN BE MYSELF.

For the LORD taketh pleasure in his people.
—PSALM 149:4 KJV

The greatest thing in the world
is to know how to be yourself.
—Michel Eyquem de Montaigne

I like to make people happy. I err on the side of mercy. I am a visionary. I am a romantic. I enjoy a good mystery. I love traditions. I would rather write a letter than talk on the phone. I have a passion for studying God's word. I don't like housework. I love to try new recipes. I must plant flowers. I am a collector. I spoil my pets.

God made each one of us with unique characteristics, talents, and abilities. Rather than try to imitate someone else, why not be who God designed us to be?

BECAUSE OF THE CROSS,
HE FINDS GOOD PLEASURE
IN ME JUST BEING MYSELF!

MY FUTURE IS SECURE.

For I am convinced that neither death nor life,
neither angels nor demons, neither the present
nor the future, nor any powers, neither height
nor depth, nor anything else in all creation,
will be able to separate us from the love
of God that is in Christ Jesus our Lord.
—ROMANS 8:38,39 NIV

To me there is something thrilling and exalting
in the thought of drifting forward into a splendid
mystery—into something that no mortal eye hath
yet seen, and no intelligence has yet declared.
—E. H. Chapin

"What if" my friends desert me? "If only" I had more education. "What if" the stock market crashes? "What if" something happens to my spouse? "If only" I had more money. "What if" I don't get the job? "If only" I were married. "What if" I can't have children?

The only "what ifs" and "if onlys" we need to be concerned about is whether or not we have the security of the Cross.

Have you found Christ? If so, be at peace!

In Him, your future is secure.

If not, don't wait until it is too late. Don't find yourself wishing, "if only" I had believed!

I CAN FORGIVE OTHERS.

Bear with each other and forgive whatever
grievances you may have against one another.
Forgive as the Lord forgave you.
—COLOSSIANS 3:13 NIV

"I can forgive, but I cannot forget," is only another
way of saying, "I will not forgive." Forgiveness
ought to be like a cancelled note—torn in two, and
burned up, so that it never can be shown against one.
—Henry Ward Beecher

Do you keep lists? A grocery list, a "honey-do" list, or a list of your daily appointments? What about a list of sins and grievances others have committed against you? Does that sound absurd? Certainly it seems ridiculous to think that we would sit down and actually compile a written list of hurts and conflicts . . . transferring last week's list forward to this week, compounding week after week, and year after year.

However, whether we do this consciously or not, we may have such a list compiling itself in our subconscious, hidden on the "hard drive" of our minds. Do you have issues, pain, and hurts that you cannot forget? Do these hurts hinder your relationship with others? There is only one way to freedom . . . forgive! If God, in His perfect holiness could forgive us . . . shouldn't we be able to forgive other imperfect human beings like ourselves? Whether old offenses or new, drag that list to the "trash bin" and push "delete."

DON'T JUST FORGIVE . . . FORGET!

MY STRENGTH IS RENEWED.

*But they that wait upon the LORD shall
renew their strength; they shall mount up
with wings as eagles; they shall run, and not
be weary; and they shall walk, and not faint.*

—ISAIAH 40:31 KJV

Strength is born in the deep silence of
long–suffering hearts; not amidst joy.

—Felicia Hemans

An eagle will always fly directly into the face of a storm. Rather than let the winds beat him back, he uses the wind to help him find the calm within the storm. Is it little wonder that this magnificent bird has to renew his strength? He will find shelter, pull out his damaged feathers, remove calcified claws, and smash his beak until it is gone. With that finished, he rests until he is renewed.

BECAUSE OF THE CROSS, WE CAN FACE LIFE'S STORMS HEAD-ON AND KNOW WE WILL BE LIFTED TO THE CALM WITHIN THEM.

And when we need to be renewed we can find shelter in the Cross, resting until once again our battered souls emerge comforted and strengthened with "wings as eagles."

I HAVE AN EXAMPLE FOR OBEDIENCE.

Going a little farther, he fell with his
face to the ground and prayed, "My Father,
if it is possible, may this cup be taken from me.
Yet not as I will, but as you will."
—MATTHEW 26:39 NIV

In all his dispensations God is at work for our good.
In prosperity he tries our gratitude; in mediocrity,
our contentment; in misfortune, our submission; in
darkness, our faith; under temptation, our steadfastness;
and at all times, our obedience and trust in him.

—John Jay

Do you ever find yourself pleading with God, "Please, *please,* don't make me do this?" Throughout the Bible, there were many who went to great lengths to try and avoid being obedient to God's will. Moses really didn't think he was capable of leading his people out of Egypt. Jonah was swallowed by a great fish when he tried to run from what God wanted him to do. Elijah got scared and ran, rather than face God's enemies the way he was supposed to.

FORTUNATELY, BECAUSE OF THE CROSS WE HAVE THE PERFECT EXAMPLE OF OBEDIENCE TO FOLLOW.

Christ was not afraid to tell His Father about the sorrow and fear He felt in facing a horrible death. The difference was that He desired to obey God's will above all else.

God hears our cries too, and has compassion for us when His will takes us beyond what we think we can bear. In His great mercy during those difficult times, He may remind us of Christ's obedience at the Cross.

I CAN OVERCOME LIFE'S CHALLENGES.

"I have told you these things, so that in me you may have peace. In this world you will have trouble. But take heart! I have overcome the world."
—JOHN 16:33 NIV

Faith makes, life proves, trials confirm,
and death crowns the Christian.
—Johann Georg Christian Hopfner

Many people have the misconception that a newly planted tree needs support of some kind against strong wind until its root system is established. Unfortunately, the root system is then compromised because the tree lacks dependence on its own roots to go deep and be strengthened by the wind. The strongest trees are found on the highest and windiest hills.

OUR OWN STRENGTH DEPENDS ON THE DEPTH OF THE CROSS IN OUR LIVES.

When we try to support ourselves through the tribulation, trials, and frustrations in the world, we will never develop the strength we need to conquer those challenges. Rely completely on the Cross and you will find the strength to overcome every storm that comes against you.

THE GRACE OF GOD INCREASES.

*And of his fulness have all we received, and grace
for grace. For the law was given by Moses,
but grace and truth came by Jesus Christ.*
—JOHN 1:16,17 KJV

Grace comes into the soul, as the morning sun
into the world; first a dawning; then a light; and
at last the sun in his full and excellent brightness.
—Thomas Adams

Every Christmas, especially when our children were little, my husband and I would wrap each child's gifts in stacks. All of the presents, wrapped individually in gold foil, were stacked with the smallest box on top, working down to the largest box on the bottom, all tied together with beautiful ribbon. On Christmas morning we would take turns opening one box after another until the final moment when we would all have that one largest box left. Together we would open our "greatest" gifts.

In the same way, God continues to give us gift upon gift. Beginning with the gift of His Son, He continues to give grace after grace, stacking up blessings for every one of His children. As a loving Father, He gives us one gift after another, until we finally receive the ultimate gift of His love . . . life forever with Him.

HIS BLESSINGS ONLY BEGIN AT THE CROSS.

Experience God's increasing, limitless grace and blessings in your life today.

ETERNITY IS REVEALED.

"Father, I want those you have given me to be with me where I am, and to see my glory, the glory you have given me because you loved me before the creation of the world."
—JOHN 17:24 NIV

The eternal world is not merely a world beyond time and the grave. It embraces time; it is ready to realize itself under all forms of temporal things. Its light and power are latent everywhere, waiting for human souls to welcome it, ready to break through the transparent veil of earthly things and to suffuse with its ineffable radiance the common life of man.

—John Caird

One afternoon, while hiking through a wooded property, I stopped to rest on the side of a hill. All I could see were immense tree trunks, dense underbrush, and scrub trees. As I made my way downhill through the lower tree limbs, underbrush, vines, and brambles, suddenly the view opened up and the beautiful tranquility of a magnificent lake was revealed.

At times, all we can see from day to day looks like scrub trees, underbrush, vines, and brambles. It seems impossible that there can be anything beyond the chaotic tangle we find ourselves in.

But because of the Cross, we can walk with Christ every day.

He leads us to the place where a magnificent view is unveiled.

ETERNITY REVEALED BEGINS AT THE CROSS.

I CAN SEE THE WORLD THROUGH GOD'S EYES.

That the God of our Lord Jesus Christ, the Father of glory, may give unto you the spirit of wisdom and revelation in the knowledge of him: The eyes of your understanding being enlightened; that ye may know what is the hope of his calling, and what the riches of the glory of his inheritance in the saints. . . .
—EPHESIANS 1:17,18 KJV

Open my eyes that I may see glimpses of truth
Thou hast for me. Open my mind that I may
read more of Thy love in word and deed.
—Clara H. Scott

Things happen in this world every day that I cannot begin to understand. For example, why do men continue to believe in lies? Why do "bad" things happen to "good" people? Why do children have to suffer? There are so many "whys"! I often cannot wait to get to heaven so I can ask God all of my "why" questions.

Yet, how often do we see a situation with an understanding that only comes from God? It may be impossible to understand everything from God's perspective, but because of the Cross I can see people, circumstances, and the world around me in a different light. The agony of childbirth that results in the miracle of a new life. A lost soul that finds Christ in the midst of tragedy. A life that is completely changed by the knowledge of God. The beauty that fills God's creation. The special uniqueness and value within every individual.

THROUGH THE CROSS, GOD ALLOWS ME TO SEE THE WORLD THOUGH HIS EYES.

I CAN BE AMONG THE CHOSEN.

For he chose us in him before the creation of the world to be holy and blameless in his sight. In love he predestined us to be adopted as his sons through Jesus Christ, in accordance with his pleasure and will.
—EPHESIANS 1:4,5 NIV

"It gives me a deep comforting sense that things seen are temporal and things unseen are eternal."
—Helen Adams Keller

Have you ever stopped to watch shoppers in the produce section of a grocery store? While trying to find the perfect fruit or vegetable, they will pick up a peach or a plum to feel for a just-ripe softness. They will thump a watermelon. They will discard an apple that is bruised or ignore cherries that are not plump enough. They will examine a tomato for shape, color, and aroma, and avoid any greens that are wilted or brown.

Whew! Isn't it wonderful that God's acceptance does not depend on our color, shape, markings, or smell?

Because of the Cross, we are chosen not for our imperfections, but for what others cannot see.

GOD LOOKS ONLY ON THE HEART.

I KNOW THE
FINAL ANSWER.

And God said unto Moses, I AM THAT I AM.
—EXODUS 3:14 KJV

*"I am the Alpha and the Omega," says
the Lord God, "who is, and who was,
and who is to come, the Almighty."*
—REVELATION 1:8 NIV

Praise God from whom all blessings flow;
Praise Him, all creatures here below;
Praise Him above, ye heavenly host;
Praise Father, Son, and Holy Ghost. Amen.

—Thomas Ken / Louis Bourgeois

Who created the universe?
Who loves me unconditionally?
Who changed the world?
Who gives all life? Who heals the sick?
Who really knows me? Who can give me comfort?
Who knows my needs? Who watches over me?
Who gives my life purpose? Who cares about me?
Who gave His life for me? Who is always with me?
Who deserves all praise? Who sets people free?
Who is always in control? Who is our lifeline?
Who conquered death on the Cross?

BECAUSE OF THE CROSS,
I KNOW THE FINAL ANSWER.

Do you know the final answer?

I CHOOSE TO SERVE THE LORD.

Choose you this day whom ye will serve . . . but
as for me and my house, we will serve the LORD.
—JOSHUA 24:15 KJV

Let death be daily before your eyes,
and you will never entertain any abject
thought, nor too eagerly covet anything.
—Epictetus

Scripture is very clear when it comes to motives. No man can serve two masters. You will love the one and hate the other. Money can be our god. Power can be our god. Acceptance can be our god. Anger can be our god. Another person can be our god. Activity can be our god. Religion can be our god. Government can be our god. Fear can be our god.

The question is, what is the reward that these gods bring? Can they save us from eternal death? Do they reach beyond our lives into eternity? Given the choice, why would we choose to serve anyone or anything other than the God that is above all other gods?

ONLY ONE CAN SAVE . . .
FIND HIM AT THE CROSS.

I AM ALWAYS LOVED.

Herein is love, not that we loved God,
but that he loved us, and sent his Son
to be *the propitiation for our sins.*

—1 JOHN 4:10 KJV

Divine love is a sacred flower, which in its early
bud is happiness, and in its full bloom is heaven.

—George William Hervey

I may roll out of bed tomorrow angry at everyone, including God. Will that change His love for me? If I raise my voice to my husband, will that change His love for me? If I do not resist a juicy piece of gossip, will that change His love for me? If I do something I know is wrong, will that change His love for me? If I forget to spend time with Him, will that change His love for me?

God loved us so much He sent his Son to die on the Cross. He loved us even though we didn't deserve it, and there is nothing I can do that will change His love for me. What wonderful truth!

I AM ALWAYS LOVED AND BECAUSE OF THE CROSS I CAN GIVE THAT LOVE TO OTHERS.

I HAVE A SYMBOL TO REMEMBER WHO I AM.

Looking unto Jesus the author and finisher of our faith; who for the joy that was set before him endured the cross, despising the shame, and is set down at the right hand of the throne of God.
—HEBREWS 12:2 KJV

The Cross of Christ, on which he was extended, points in the length of it, to heaven and earth, reconciling them together; and in the breadth of it, to former and following ages, as being equally salvation to both.
—Samuel Rutherford

How often do you see a cross? A significant and sacred symbol of Christ's love for us, we have almost become numb to its true meaning because of today's commercialism. We find crosses on churches, memorials, Christian Bibles and books, T-shirts, baseball caps, handbags, briefcases, stationery, watches, necklaces, rings, wall plaques, door knockers, bumper stickers, dishes, candles, holiday decorations, cookie cutters, wallpaper, record labels, and more . . . a vast array of items bearing a symbol that has endured for two thousand years.

The next time you look upon a cross, stop to remember Christ's birth, life, death, and resurrection. Because of the selfless price He paid on our behalf, the Cross is significant.

REMEMBER WHAT HE DID AND WHO YOU ARE *BECAUSE OF THE CROSS*.

ABOUT THE AUTHOR

Beverly Courrege is the author of the runaway bestseller *WWJD: Answers to What Would Jesus Do*. Her most recent titles are *Yield to Jesus; Y2J* and *The Joy of Resurrection*.

Photography by C. David Edmonson

Beverly has been active in the Christian gift and book industry for more than 25 years as co-owner of Courrege Design, a Christian gift manufacturer. As a designer, she has created hundreds of items for the Christian marketplace, and she actively writes for newspapers, magazines, trade publications, and movie reviews.

Beverly and her husband, Boo, have a grown son, daughter, and son-in-law and live in the Dallas Metroplex.

Additional copies of this book and other titles
by RiverOak Publishing are available
from your local bookstore.

If you have enjoyed this book, or if it has impacted
your life, we would like to hear from you.
Please contact us at:

RiverOak Publishing
Department E
P.O. Box 700143
Tulsa, Oklahoma 74170-0143
Or by e-mail at info@riveroakpublishing.com

RIVER
OAK
PUBLISHING